What's Your Dream?

The 21-Day Morning Routine

By Michael J Gilbert

What's Your Dream?

The 21-Day Morning Routine

Copyright © 2016 by Michael J Gilbert

www.whatsyourdreammorningroutine.com

www.wydmr.com

All rights reserved. No part of this book may be reproduced or transmitted in any form or by any means without written permission from the author, Michael J Gilbert

ISBN 978-0-9996626-3-2

Cover created with Lynn Hasday, Graphic Designer lynnhasday.com (thanks for your support time on this project Lynn) and Michael J Gilbert

Thanks to Michele Preisendorf, Senior Editor and Administrative Assistant at Eschler Editing: Award-winning editing, design, production & promotion services for authors, publishers, and organizations, for the editing. (note: post edit errors created by Michael J. Gilbert)

"It's human nature to explore, start with yourself. What's Your Dream?"

— MWW (Michael's Words of Wisdom)

The more we are ourselves the happier we become. The happier we become the more we will experience living our dreams. This book is daily exercises of being loving, compassionate, joyful and at peace with oneself. This is how we become more of ourself. As we create more value and appreciation of being ourselves we instinctually create, manifest and share our dreams with the world. This also increases and elevates our level of happiness.

Here are five reasons why this book works as an exercise to create and manifest your dreams of health, wealth, and relationships:

THE DECISION

ROUTINE TO SELF-IMAGE

SELF-CARE TO WARM-HEARTED

VISUALIZING TO BELIEVING

SELF-CONFIDENCE TO COMMUNITY INVOLVEMENT

1. The most important part of creating our dreams is our <u>decision</u> to do so. This decision is really valuing ourself and others as a human beings. With the daily exercises in this book we can strengthen our positive self-image and self-value to support our decision to create and manifest our dreams to share with the world. Only you can create and manifest your dreams and it starts with your decision to do so.

2. Doing a morning routine for twenty one days creates a new self-image with greater self-value of being yourself. With our intention of be loving, joyful, compassionate and content with our own innate natural talents our self-image will grow from the unlimited potential of love, joy, compassion and content. This will develop a self-image with unlimited potential to live your dreams.

3. Doing self-care every day for twenty-one days creates a self-image of being compassionate. Being compassionate with ourselves and other will develop a warm heart. Cultivating a warm heart for the *process* of creating and manifesting our dreams is an exercise in sharing a warm heart. As we exercise our warm-heartedness we will also develop the strength to share warm-heartedness with the people and the world we live in.

4. Visualizing your dreams is a necessary step to creating your dreams. What's Your Dream Morning Routine has space to write out your dreams and also includes the opportunity The more we love our dreams the clearer and more believable our dreams become. Believing in our dreams is one of the keys to creating our dreams. Before anyone else will believe in your dreams you have to believe in your dreams.

5. Self-confidence to be yourself is the seed that grows into community involvement. What's Your Dream Morning Routine includes exercises to expand and grow our value of who we are as a person. This is the foundation that will grow our self-confidence. Creating our dreams to share with our community amplifies the fun of creating our dreams. Having fun and supporting our community while creating our dreams will inspire us to repeat this process as well as learning to support others in creating and manifesting their dreams.

Why face a fear? Why heal oneself?

In 2016 I found myself living in my car. Things did not look like they were going to get better. This book was written while living in my car. I decided to learn more about love, compassion, joy, content and gratitude because I was not living an enjoyable life to share with people. From this decision came the research and development of What's Your Dream Morning Routine. (WYDMR) and my desire to share this book with people who like to invest in being more themselves.

Thanks very much for your interest in this book.
With kindness
Michael J Gilbert, BSN, Certified Happiness Pioneer

Happiness Ninja Skills =   Self-Expression

"All our dreams come true from happiness, not the other way around."

— MWW (Michael's Words of Wisdom)

Table of Contents

Appreciation 9
Know Thyself 12
Ask "Why?"—Create Focus 21
WYD? Morning Routine Outline 26
What's Your Dream? Morning Routine 27
1 Water Your Body, Grow Your Happiness 31
2 Practice Self-Care, Learn Compassion 34
3 Breathe Slowly, Slow Down........................... 38
4 Smile While Breathing Slowly 40
5 Self-Commitment 42
6 What I Love about other people and Why .. 46
7 What I Am Grateful for and Why 49
8 Whom and How I Will Serve Today, Why..... 57
9 Ask "What Would It Take?" 67
10 Reward Yourself for Doing WYDMR 74
The End of WYDMR: Let The River Flow 80
Letting Go of Homelessness 83

Please NOTE: pages 82-173 are mostly blank journaling pages so you can write your answers of the questions on each page for twenty-one days.

1. If I was ten-times happier, If I was one-hundred times happier, what would I be doing, what would my dreams be for myself?...............86
2. What part of my innate goodness; love, joy, compassion and peace, would I like to exercise to support my dreams coming true?......................89
3. How will being: loving, joyful, compassionate, and/or peaceful, support sharing my creations with humanity? 92

What's Your Dream Morning Routine.............95–178
References 180
MWW (Michael's Words of Wisdom).................... 187

Appreciation
Because People Living Their Dreams Have Inspired Me to Be More Myself

There are many people who have influenced the creation of this book. Jack Canfield, for one, who said, "if you can't find the book you are looking for, it means you are supposed to write it." (VR1) For many years I struggled with depression and found depression support groups were not for me. What I found beneficial was happiness support groups, except they are not called happiness support groups by name. Happiness support groups are groups that share a common interest in something the group loves, like snowboarding, biking, hiking, business startups, art, science, nature, writing, reading, or any common interest. Thus, the actual creation of happiness often gets overlooked or taken for granted. I wrote this book to create more awareness of creating happiness on purpose, with intention. Writing this book has helped me to value myself as a human being and thus appreciate all people more sincerely. Yet most of my inspiration has come from other people who live and share a life of their dreams. The inspiring life these people have created for themselves is an example that we all can create and manifest our dreams. This is why I'm grateful for people living their dreams.

Much appreciation to Oprah Winfrey and Shawn Achor for their online curse: "21 days to happiness." I went through this course while writing this book and found it to be a good happiness support group that has been influential and supportive in writing this book. I am also grateful for the following people who have inspired me by sharing their happiness. Much love and thanks to Will Smith, Jim Carrey, Tom Cruise, Jeremy Jones, Chris Anthony, Sierra Quitquit, Jamie Anderson, Lindsey Vonn, Mikaela Shiffrin, Tom Bilyeu, Gregg Braden, Dr Brene Brown, Brendon Burchard, Deepak Chopra, Marie Forleo, Michelle Gielan, Dave Goggins, Lewis Howes, Byron Katie, HH XIV Dalai Lama, Dan Millman, Stefan Pylarinos, Tony Robbins, Christy Marie Sheldon, Elkhart Tolle, Linsey Sterling, Dr Tom Hackett, my Tai Chi classes, Yoga classes, and my family and friends. Thanks for sharing the good times.

CERTIFICATE OF SUCCESS

This certifies that

Michael J. Gilbert

has successfully completed 21 Days to a Happier Life with Shawn Achor, and is officially a Hoopie at Home. Thank you for embracing a happier life for yourself and for everyone you touch.

Awarded by

Saturday July 30th, 2016

"Know Thyself"
Knowing Thyself is Knowing How to Create Happiness

Ever notice how animals live instinctively? Birds, alligators, bears, deer, fish, whales—all wild animals live very instinctively. One of the differences between humans and animals is that animals know instinctively what and who they are going to be when they grow up, and humans don't. Humans can grow up to be doctors, communicators, scientists, artists, athletes, entrepreneurs, cooks, naturalists, musicians, athletes… anything that inspires us. Humans have to choose what to be when we grow up. Now that many of our basic needs; food, shelter, clothing—are met and we add technology, we have nearly eliminated our need to act and live instinctively. Not living from our instincts, we are living from how society shows and tells us how to act. The media, family, friends, and our social surroundings create our beliefs and influence to even dictate how we should live. Much of our media and society beliefs are based on competition and conflict. Today we are becoming more aware and supportive of each other and our environment. And together rather than individually we can better support nature around us and within us, like our own individual natural talents.

If we lived in a time and place without food and shelter we would instinctively build shelter and find food. But because our instinctive needs are provided, we look outside of ourselves for what we should be doing. And we live in a society with false beliefs, like "Working hard is good for you." The truth is, doing things you enjoy is good for you. Some people may say that if people only did things they enjoyed, nothing would get done. Yet when people go on vacation and have fun, they often expend twice as much energy than they normally do and come home from vacation needing a rest before going back to work. This book is a daily practice to create value in who you are, what you enjoy, and what you would like to share with the world. To simplify, lets look at a question by Bruce Lee, "How can I express myself totally and completely?" (VD 2) Bruce Lee has also said in a more direct way, "How can I be me?" (VD 3)

The exercises in this book are designed to support a person being themselves more honestly and openly by asking them to write, speak, to create clarity and increased awareness of what they love. From this awareness, we can more consciously do and share what we love with intention. Sharing what we love is a form of self-expression that creates happiness. The exercises in this book are designed to support you creating this experience for yourself.

Let's go into more detail on of what this book is about —being more yourself. This book is designed to provide you with a daily morning exercises to create awareness, love and appreciation of who you are, as well as a focus of sharing this love with the world. These are the actions that support a person's happiness and will guide your life into your dreams. This is creating happiness with intention.

Let's take a look at intention: in-ten-tion /in'ten(t)SH(e)n/

1. "**Intention is a mental state that represents a commitment to carrying out an action or actions in the future. Intention involves mental activities such as planning and forethought.**" (https://en.wikipedia.org/wiki/Intention) (WR 1)
2. "**An intentional action is a function to accomplish a desired goal and is based on the belief that the course of action will satisfy a desire.**" (https://en.wikipedia.org/wiki/Intention) (WR 1)
3. For the purpose of this book let's call intention *a person's decision to proactively create a way of being in this moment.* We are all human "beings" and this book is an outline to proactively create a happier way of "being" in this moment.

If you want to be happy, try asking yourself, "*Why* do I want to be happy?" To practice the intention to be happy, ask questions to increase awareness of what inspires you. For example, a golfer may ask the question, "How can I hit the ball on the green?" A man or woman who wants to have a family may ask, "How can I be a parent or spouse?" A homeless person may ask, "How can I live in a house?" By asking questions, we create intention. Another example: ask, "What would it take to _____?" We are not necessarily asking ourselves this question. Ask the question and be open to the answer coming from anyone or anyplace. Be open to noticing the answer as it presents itself.

This morning routine requires that you practice being more aware of your feelings and experiences of happiness each day. Whether a person becomes happier or not is not as important as *noticing* whether we become happier or not. What gets rewarded gets repeated, and noticing yourself becoming happier is a reward for the actions of your intentions that created your happiness.

Now, let's look at a few thoughts on happiness:

- "Happiness is not something ready ready-made, it comes from your own actions."

  —HH XIV Dalai Lama (BR 1)

- "Real happiness in life starts when you begin to cherish others."

  —Lama Zopa Rinpoche (WR 2)

- "Happiness comes from developing a skill."
                                    —Allen Watts
- "Happiness is when what you think, what you say, and what you do are all in harmony."
                                    —Mahatma Gandhi (BR 2)
- "Happiness is the joy you feel moving towards your potential."
                                    —Shawn Achor. (WR 3)
- "The happiness you feel is in direct proportion to the love you give."
                                    —Oprah Winfrey. (WR 4)
- "Happiness or unhappiness comes from how a person is "being" with their moment."
   —Michael J Gilbert (Michael's Words of Wisdom, MWW)
- "Happiness is recognizing your true self as space, emptiness, unlimited potential."
                                    —Michael J. Gilbert

Notice that most of these definitions of happiness state that happiness is a result of your actions. *This book is daily exercises to create more awareness and appreciation of the natural characteristics that make you—you.* We do this with exercises of being loving, compassionate, joyful and at peace with ourself. This new and greater level of self awareness and appreciation is where we create and manifest our dreams and become more ourself.

The exercises in this book are designed to create the intention of "being" how a person wants to be in the present moment. When we act from intention, we create our way of being in this moment, rather than reacting to what is going on around us.

"In 1948 the World Health Organization (WHO) defined health as "a state of complete physical, mental, and social well-being and not merely the absence of disease or infirmity." Other definitions have been proposed, among which is a recent definition that correlates health and personal satisfaction. (WR 5) For the purpose of this book, health can also be seen as a reflection of a person's happiness.

Wikipedia describes wealth as "an especially important part of social stratification." (WR 6) And our social connections can be a significant part of our happiness. Therefore we can see a desire for wealth also as a desire for another kind of social connection. I believe this is one of the best reasons to pursue wealth—because we are social beings and being social is one of our greatest opportunities for happiness.

As has everyone who's ever lived, I have struggled through some difficult times of unhappiness. Change started to take place as I developed my intention to be happy and became curious of my suffering. Then came the humbling awareness that I, and only I, created my unhappiness. By taking full responsibility for both my unhappiness and creating my unhappiness, I am also able to take full responsibility for my happiness and creating my happiness.

The practice of creating happiness with intention will bring up challenges of our old beliefs, like "Things are hard," or "I should be unhappy because _____," or "I am angry/unhappy/fearful because of that other person." What I have noticed is that these thoughts are not the problem. What creates more suffering than the thought "I am not enough" is in how we treat this thought. By being angry with this thought it will only become more painful. By stepping back from our thoughts and noticing how we feel while thinking different thoughts we can start to see how we create our own suffering with feelings we create associated to our thoughts. What if we try creating space for the suffering of our fears, deepest anger, or most painful emotions by observing how we create and react to these thoughts and feelings

One of the keys in this book to creating and manifesting our dreams is asking yourself the question **WHY**? For example, if you like something about yourself then ask *why?* Asking questions creates reasons to invest in things you like and love about yourself. The more we know and care for ourself the more we will "be" and express ourself.

"Develop a routine of valuing yourself and your dreams and one day you will be living them."
—*MWW*

Will Smith once said, "You don't set out to build a brick wall, you set out to lay a brick as perfectly as a brick can be laid and one day you will have a wall." (Will Smith interview 60 Minutes VR4) WYD Morning Routine is about creating happiness in this moment. The more moments we create happiness, the more we can look back and see our happy life.

"All our dreams come true from happiness, not the other way around."
—*MWW*

When getting into this book and deciding to develop a daily practice of creating and manifesting your dreams, be prepared—it takes effort before it becomes effortless. When we ask "*why*" we would we invest in creating our dreams, the answer is; "The purpose of life is to be happy" HH XIV Dalai Lama. (WR 7) Therefore, investing time in and value in one's dreams is fulfilling your life's purpose to be happy.

As Happiness Researcher Shawn Achor says, "Happiness actually fuels success not the other way around." (VR5) This means happy people are successful due to their happiness. The belief that happiness comes from success is an illusion created to keep people striving for "more" so that we will *then* be happy. Working for happiness to come after success is the proverbial carrot many of us chase.

There is one last thing before we go into practicing a morning routine of loving, caring and being more yourself. Increasing either our level of happiness or our level of unhappiness can cause anxiety. This has been found in psychology and in my own experience. Support from the people around us can ease the transition to a happier state of being. Be sure you are comfortable with any support you may receive.

It creates an initial sense vulnerability to raise a person's level of happiness. Recognizing this with kindness is a good place to start. I have also found that exercise supports a person ability to rest and during rest is when we accept a higher level of happiness. If the mind is anxious or excited and the body is inactive, the body will not need as much rest as the mind. Exercise helps a person rest by giving the body more need for rest. Then the body and mind can rest together.

Ask "Why?" —Create Focus
Creating and Manifesting Our Dreams Takes Determination, Effort and Action

My life has been fairly normal, other than not yet having married. I grew up with two brothers, moved around quite a bit—from California, to Washington, and back to California—finished high school in and went to college in Colorado, and worked as a RN for eleven years. Then things went south as I developed severe depression and faced significant challenges in 2005. I lost my job as an RN, lived in a group home for people experiencing mental challenges, worked multiple jobs, and lost multiple jobs. Then things started getting better in 2010. I moved in with some friends and got back to doing some of the things I enjoyed with people who also enjoyed those things, like snowboarding, running, and mountain biking. Yet my roller-coaster life continued, and in 2016, I found myself living in my car. Things did not look like they were going to get any better.

I wrote this book while living in my car and deciding to live an inspiring life no matter what. From this decision came the research and development of *What's Your Dream?*

the 21-day morning routine. This decision also grew my inspiration to share this book with people who are inspired to live their dreams by being more themselves.

So how can we be more of ourself? What if we were more loving, compassionate, joyful, at peace? If being this way was our intention than in doing so we could say we are being more ourself. What if these four thoughts are who we are? Then when we we are being loving or compassionate we can say we are and being ourself.

Now let's look at who we think we are. Some people may say we are our personalities, our strengths, the way we are that is different from everyone else. What if we look at our personality, strengths, our body, mind emotions as what we are experiencing and who we really are is love, joy, compassion and content. Then by being loving, joyful, compassionate, or content with our personality traits like artistic, logical, musical for example, we are supporting our human experience by being more of ourselves, more loving, joyful, compassionate and content.

Now that we know who we are, let's look at the question "What is my dream?" I have incorporated three questions for you to answer before starting WYDMR. These questions help create focus and clarity while doing WYDMR. These questions are designed to help a person answers the question, "What is my dream?" to create clarity and focus on what you would like to create and manifest in your life.

These questions are written in this book with space to answer before starting WYDMR. Your answers to these questions will support your focus each morning while doing What's Your Dream—Morning Routine. I've provided space to write your answers of these questions in this book. And there is also space to write in this book while doing WYDMR each day.

The first question is **"If I was ten times happier, If I was one-hundred times happier, what would I be doing, what would my dreams be for myself?"** Think of yourself as a radiating light of happiness that brightens everything and everyone around you. Then answer this question, "What would I be doing? What would my dreams be for myself?"—with the state of mind of being one-hundred times happier. Answer this question with your lifetime in mind. What experiences in life would you invest in creating? What inspire you? —spirituality, art, science, communication, nature, social, family, health (mental, physical, emotional), or general well-being? Simply focus on how you would be inspired to live as a person that is one hundred times happier than you are right now.

The second question is, **"What part of my innate goodness; love, joy, compassion and peace—would I like to expand my understanding of to support my dreams**

coming true?" We can develop our unlimited potential by practicing these four thoughts of love, joy, compassion and peace. Therefore, if a person's dream is to create happiness by doing art, the second question is, "How can I express; love, joy, compassion or peace while creating art?" This question now becomes a very individual question. Which one of the four immeasurable thoughts will support your expression of art? Which one of the four thoughts; love, joy, compassion, or peace, would you enjoy experiencing while doing art?

Let's go a little more into the four immeasurable thoughts. Here is my definition of the four thoughts; these do not necessarily need to be yours. These definitions are based on my understanding and study of these thoughts and also support answering the questions later in this book.

- Love: The wish for all beings to be happy.
- Joy: The happiness that is free from suffering.
- Compassion: The wish for all beings to be free from suffering.
- Content: The freedom of allowing everyone and everything to be just as it is, peaceful happiness.

When a person knows the areas that inspire them, such as—spirituality, art, science, communication, nature, social, family, health, or general well-being—then the second question is asking, "How am I expressing love, joy, compassion, or peace through my interest?

When a person feels health is a strong part of their personal interest, something of value and focus, then asking "how can I create peaceful happiness while investing in health?" This will create the intention to be more content with one's health.

And the third question is, **"How will being: loving, joyful, compassionate, and or content with my personality and strengths support sharing my dreams with humanity?"** The more we invest in our personalities and strengths with love, joy, compassion and content, the more comfortable and easier it will be to share ourselves with the people around us. This is a way to develop self-confidence. This can also support our greatest source of happiness, social connection.

Answering these three questions before starting this 21-days of WYDMR will help you create a focus each morning as you answer the daily questions in WYDMR. When you take the time to write these questions down, they will stay in your memory better. You will also have the answers available to review before doing WYDMR each morning. See pages 78–84, where you'll find space to write your answers.

Investing in your intention to be happy takes courage. This is the courage to let go the belief we are our thoughts feelings beliefs and investing in being loving, joyful, compassionate and content with our personality, beliefs, thoughts and feelings. Through this change we will become a happier person by developing a new way to treat ourselves. May the force be with you. Let's get started!

WYDMR Outline
The Daily Routine Outlined

- 1: Drink Water 24-60 oz second thing after awakening
- 2: Self-Care 3-5 minutes
- 3: Slow Breathing: Three minutes while smiling
- 4: Write: What do I love about myself and others? Why?
- 5: Write: What I am grateful for? Why?
- 6: Write: Who am I going to serve today? Why?
- 7: Self-Commitment: Notice yourself doing WYDMR and write in ten words or less what you have noticed about yourself as a result of doing this morning routine.
- 8: Laugh out loud and cultivate a warm heart and appreciation while reading what you have written for the day doing WYDMR and investing in creating your dreams.

What's Your Dream Morning Routine
Like a Song, a dance, a Routine Needs a Beginning, Middle, and End

In the outline for What's Your Dream Morning Routine, there is a beginning, middle, and end. This is very important. A morning routine is just that: an exercise done first thing in the morning to create an intention for the day, and completed. Like song, dance, meditation practice, gymnastics routine, stopping in the middle would make these actions feel scattered and incomplete. Your intention for the day would not have focus. When doing your morning routine, prepare to start the morning routine, do it, then end it. Like pouring a glass of water once you are done doing WYDMR it's done, now go on with your day. Once the day is over, it may be beneficial to go back to your notes to see how your intention affected your day. But going back to a morning routine during the day could turn a morning routine into a continuous distraction throughout the day. This would be giving too much time and attention to the morning routine. A morning routine is best served as a way to set an intention for how you would like to express yourself during your day.

Set up WYDMR as your morning routine. Make it your own. Set up your morning routine to be ready first thing in the morning. Prepare to do WYDMR like a musician, athlete, dancer, artist, cook, or scientist prepares to perform an activity.

Plan to complete this morning routine in twenty minutes or less. Do this by practicing doing WYDMR for a day or two before starting your twenty-one-day exercise. If twenty minutes is too much time to commit to for twenty-one days, then do only do the writing portion of the routine. Set a goal to complete the routine in fifteen minutes or less. It is more important to do the routine consistently for twenty-one days than to do a routine that allows some things to be missed on some days. Demand consistency of yourself. Twenty-one is a magic number when creating a new self-image, and consistency is the key.

Developing a stronger intention to be happy can paradoxically bring up emotions like anger or fear. These emotions can lead to procrastination and missing a day. With determination, the exercises of investing in yourself will help expand your comfort zone of being happy.

This morning routine is also about relieving our own suffering. I learned a *key to relieving suffering* from Gregg Braden, who says, "*Blessing whatever causes the suffering.*" (BR 3) It is very common to look at this quote and think of people, places, things, or events that have caused or cause us pain. But what really causes our pain is our personality, intellect, and our feelings of anger, jealousy, loneliness, depression, anxiety, and wanting something to be different. These are our inner pains and are the feelings and beliefs that need our blessing. For our blessing to be more directed to our suffering of feelings, thoughts, and beliefs, let's say, "I bless the causes of my suffering." With the understanding that our own anger, fear, jealousy, pride, desire, and beliefs of separation cause our suffering, not other people or events.

A person does not change oneself; a person changes how they treat themselves.

—MWW

While doing WYDMR, when feelings such as anger, loneliness, anxiety, or any painful experiences arise, say, "I bless the cause of my suffering." When noticing a belief that other people are against you, things won't change, or life is hard, say, "I bless the causes of my suffering." Bless your painful beliefs and feelings. Do this at any time during the next twenty-one days. "I bless the causes of my suffering." You are acknowledging that you are the creator of both your own suffering and happiness. And blessing our anger is a practice of self-compassion.

"I bless the causes of my happiness."

—*MWW*

This is my favorite part of my book, blessing the causes of our happiness. Blessing the causes of our suffering is self-compassion. And blessing the causes of our happiness is self-love. This is important because if we are free of suffering without happiness we will go back to suffering. By blessing the causes of our happiness, we are also creating a reason to be free of suffering. We can then enjoy happiness even more.

Now, take note of your thoughts and feelings while doing WYDMR. Hear yourself bless the causes of suffering and happiness and notice the different feelings from doing both of these blessings. Also notice your intentions for both blessings. See if you can notice how they complement each other.

Each of the following chapters is an outline of each step in this morning routine. These outlines will create a clear understanding of how each step can create happiness and be developed from your own interest of what you would like to experience and how you would like to grow as a person.

1

Water Your Body, Grow Your Happiness
Creating Health Creates Happiness

Because good physical health supports happiness, drink more water. Water is the greatest part of our body, anywhere from 45–90 percent depending on our age.

Drinking ample amounts of water can support and improve our body's health more than any other single source of nutrition. And being free of physical pain creates space for happiness to grow. A healthy body will tolerate pain and illness easier and heal faster than an unhealthy body. A healthy body opens the door to greater happiness. This step of WYDMR is for your physical health.

In this step, decide on a specific amount of water to drink first thing in the morning for the twenty-one days

of this morning routine. Drink a minimum of 24–60 ounces of water. When deciding on how to personalize this morning routine for yourself, be sure to stick to a set routine for twenty-one days before making any changes.

When we are born, our bodies are approximately 75 percent water. By the time we reach seventy years of age, that amount has decreased to approximately 50 percent water (WR 8). If a person increased their percentage of water by even just 1 percent, how would they feel? Younger, healthier, and more energized? Water supports every chemical reaction in the body. Chemical reactions are what create energy. This is why water is so important in how we feel—water facilitates creating energy.

These first steps in What's Your Dream Morning Routine are based on physical self-care, and drinking water is caring for our physical body. Using a pitcher with a filter is an affordable way to take the chlorine and other chemicals out of drinking water and improve its taste. Watering down fruit juice or adding minerals to water can also make water more palatable. Water without sugar is recommended for this step. Make a habit of drinking water first (or second) thing in the morning. Do whatever it takes to be successful in this step—add lemon, minerals (like Himalayan rock salt or other mineral salts), or filter your water so you're more likely to drink lots. Please do not use coffee. Coffee is very acidic and is a stimulant that can be addicting, and addictions do not support happiness.

Drinking water enhances the benefits of anything we put into our bodies for our health by supporting digestion and absorption. I have found alkaline water to be beneficial in softening muscle aches, supporting mental alertness, suppressing appetite, and increasing hydration. Alkaline water is now available in many grocery stores, and there are now devices that make tap water alkaline.

What gets rewarded gets repeated, so note how your body feels both before starting this routine and twenty-one days after. Enjoying better physical health is a reward if we make the intention to notice our improved physical health.

"Creating health creates happiness."
—*MWW*

One last thing we can add to water before drinking is our gratitude, love, joy, compassion, content, dreams and prayers. Talking to our water this way before drinking supports embodying our dreams with a positive intention. For another view of talking to water look at: "Speaking to the Water" by Uplift, December 11, 2017 on youtube.

2

Practice Self-Care —Learn Compassion

Our Happiness Is Dependent on How We Treat Ourselves and Others, and How We Treat Others Is a Reflection of How We Treat Ourselves

When the air pressure in a plane is lost and the oxygen mask drops and we put the mask on ourselves first before assisting others with theirs. Caring for ourselves so that we can care for others is the root of this part of What's Your Dream Morning Routine.

"Does our intention come from how we treat our suffering?"

—MWW

What if how we treat our own suffering of anger, jealousy, loneliness, pride, fear, desire, or other types of suffering, is also the root of how we develop our intention to be happy? For example; if I don't like the pain of loneliness and react to this feeling with anger, how will this affect interactions with people who notice my feelings of loneliness? If I treat loneliness with care and with an appreciation of my desire to connect with people, how will this affect the way I interact with people? Could we develop happiness if the way we manage our suffering actually relieves suffering at its core? Can a person get closer to relieving their suffering at its core by practicing self-compassion every morning for three minutes?

In this step of WYDMR, you choose something that is soothing or important in your daily life to take care of in a way that is also enjoyable.

For example, my teeth are prone to decay, so in this step, I care for my teeth. Sometimes I notice the compassion in caring for my teeth, or my love of health. Noticing the act of self-care is as important as doing the self-care. This is noticing your innate goodness and compassion.

This step should be a physical act of self-care done for three to five minutes to keep the time of the total morning routine down to twenty minutes or less.

Self-care, as in a thirty-minute run, is not part of this routine. A morning routine only becomes beneficial if it is done every single day. Limiting the time required to do

WYDMR will make it easier to do every day. Doing a morning routine is a great way to proactively create your life. Start with twenty-one days and notice the benefits at the end of the twenty-one days as a reward. Creating a new self-image, from doing a morning routine to create and manifest your dreams, is more important than living our dreams. This is because living enjoyably is more important then living our dreams. When we are enjoying life, creating and manifesting our dreams will also be enjoyable. If a person is not happy with their self-image and not enjoying life, creating and manifesting dreams will also not be fullfilling.

When doing self-care, choose something that will be enjoyable to do and create enjoyable results. Notice what you appreciate about the self-care you have decided on. What can you learn about yourself, related to the kind of self-care that you like?

Suggestions for three to five minute self-care: washing your face, washing your feet, foot massage, oral care, crunches, laughing, dancing, facial massage, one or two favorite yoga poses, stretching, running in place, making your bed, hand massage, massaging an area of chronic pain, holding your arms straight up over head in a V (this is a universal sign of victory and creates happiness), massaging your cheeks to support smiling, burpees, or brushing your hair. This exercise is self-care for your body.

This needs to be a physical act of care. Sitting in a massage chair or lying in the sun are not acts of *doing*. Make this a moment of self-care.

Every day while practicing self-care, notice *why* you're practicing this care. For example, if my self-care is brushing my teeth to prevent cavities, I am noticing how I care for my teeth and support myself by keeping my teeth clean. I'm also noticing additional benefits, like fresh breath. Notice a different positive aspect of the self-care you're practicing every day.

3

Breathe Slowly, Slow Down
Rushing our Dreams Pushes Them into the Future

This part of the morning routine is to be done while smiling (to be discussed in next chapter). Slow, deep inhaling and exhaling is common in yoga, meditation, tai chi, and other types of moving and non-moving meditation.

slowing our breathing takes focus and the intention to inhale and exhale slowly. This shows us we can create experiences with intention. Focus on slow, deep breaths that each last about four seconds. Think of feeling your breathing with curiosity. Notice you can feel your body breathing. Have you ever become curious about this experience? What is it that enables us to focus and feel our breath? Being curious can support being aware of our breath without creating tension our stress.

This step of WYD? morning routine is focusing on slowly inhaling and exhaling for three minutes. Start with three minutes. This may seem like a short time and that is the idea. A second or third three minutes can be added later. Learning to focus is difficult and interval training is the fastest way to make a change. For example, if a person wants to learn to run a mile faster, they can either run one mile a day for five days a week for a month, or break up the training to running four quarter miles or eight eighths of a mile five days a week for a month. Breaking things down to smaller parts makes things easier and has been shown to create better results.

Interval training has been studied in physical training more than mental training, yet I have found it to be true in my experience for both mental and physical endeavors. For WYDMR, start by focusing on your breathing for one minute, and do this three times for a total of three minutes. Just focus on the act of breathing or the feeling of breathing. This will support the intention to increase and improve a person's ability to focus.

4

Smile While Breathing Slowly
Smiling Creates Happiness Now

This step in WYDMR is done in combination with the last step of slow breathing for three minutes. These two steps are a three-minute exercise done simultaneously.

If your intention is to be happy, then be happy. What's Your Dream Morning Routine is a way to focus on the moment. Smiling right now for three minutes is living your intention to be happy. Smiling releases chemicals in our brain related to happiness, so this practice is for our mind and body. Look at what happens in these three minutes. Notice how you feel. Smiling and breathing is done for only three minutes, rather than ten or fifteen, to create the practice of a strong focus without distractions of thoughts, feelings or other amusing things.

In Dr. Ronald E. Riggio's article in *Psychology Today* (June 2, 2012) "There's Magic in Your Smile; How smiling affects your brain." (BR 4) he writes that smiling fights stress, and releases neuropeptides and dopamine endorphins. These enzymes function in the body as pain relievers, antidepressants, lower blood pressure, and make a person better looking. So what's not to smile about?

Another benefit of doing a morning routine comes from the daily practice. One day, after I had been doing a morning routine for about forty to fifty days, I had a very stressful conversation and found myself quite upset over a disagreement with a coworker. With my practice of smiling every day, I decided to smile until I was not upset anymore. Thus I have found this morning routine gives you the tools to decide to be happy in difficult situations.

How can deciding to smile change your life? Same as a decision to create and manifest your dreams. Also as a decision to create a new more lovable self image. By acting with intention to support our decisions we are embracing our decision to be a person who lives the life of our dreams.

If faced with a stressful situation, how would lowering your blood pressure, or decreasing depression and pain, or becoming better looking help the situation? If nothing else, at least becoming better looking is fun! This is why we add smiling to the step of slow, deep breathing for three minutes—for the fun of it!

5

Self-Commitment: Notice Yourself Doing WYDMR

Self-Commitment Is Being Loving, Joyful, Compassionate, Content, Grateful, and noticing this.

"The road to success is paved with commitment."
—*Will Smith (VR 6)*

Performing a morning routine is a commitment to yourself. Being the source of your happiness is the only answer to true happiness. **Take one to two minutes to notice yourself doing a morning routine to create a new way of treating yourself.** Notice the value you're putting into your intention to value how your treating yourself and those close to you. Notice possible benefits for yourself and the people close to you by investing in yourself to have a great day! Noticing a commitment to yourself and your happiness is a reward for doing WYDMR.

Now, how about a reality check? We all have our comfort levels of being happy and unhappy. Doing a morning routine will disrupt our current comfort level of who we think we are. Thus we run into procrastination, thinking up reasons to skip a day. We may experience anger, feelings of insecurity, and disruption in relationships or work. When these or other things come up and make doing a morning routine difficult, we need to exercise determination. Determination to make our life more loving, joyful, compassionate and at peace—is like a compass that guides our actions. Yet what is determination, really? How can we create determination? Is determination enough?

To write this book, I invested in Shawn Achor and Oprah Winfrey's "21 Days to a Happier Life." (WR 9) I completed the course and became a "certified happiness pioneer." I also asked for feedback on my book from a local entrepreneur group that inspired me to invest in a graphic designer for the cover and editing. I did these things while still living in my car. I also spent money on weekend entrepreneur seminars to learn how to create a business around my book. My continued determination led to a job that included housing, insurance, and an income that allowed me to afford skiing and snowboarding in the winter. Yet at the end of this winter, I was suffering from depression again.

Quite simply I was focusing on enjoying my life as a professional again. Having worked as an RN the lifestyle and people I interacted with were quite different than driving jobs that I had been working. Being dependent on something outside of ourself for happiness sets ourself up for unhappiness.

So this 21-day exercise is a practice of self-love, joy, compassion, contentment and gratitude. Writing every morning about what a person appreciates about themselves and applying love, joy, compassion and content for ourself is how we become more of ourself. for example if being artistic, athletic, logical or scientific is part of our personality as a person, being loving, joyful, compassionate or content with this part of our personality will support and grow this aspect of ourself. By being and growing ourself with love, joy, compassion and content we more naturally create and manifest our dreams. This process works because our dreams are actually a reflection of how we would like to see ourselves. Whatever we want in life is a reflection of how we wish to see ourself. If we want amazing health and fitness we want to see ourself as a person who enjoys health and fitness activities. So part of this morning exercise would include appreciation of our health. Also we could practice content and focus while exercising. If we wish to be a politician we want to love interacting and communicating with people. And our morning exercise could include compassion for our efforts to communicate with many different people and the challenges of creating connections with people having multiple types of backgrounds.

The more we inquire within ourself with questions, awareness of what we like, and apply love, compassion, joy and content to who we are, the more self-confidence we will create in who we are. Here are some questions to think about and create short answers.

- Can you see yourself as a happier person?

- Imagine sharing what you love. How would learning more about yourself support this?

- Who would you like to share your dreams with?

6

Write: What I Love About Others and Why? (one to three minutes.)

Would writing about what you love every morning give your life more sense of direction and meaning?

"Know Thyself, Appreciate Thyself, and Grow."

—*MWW*

This is the first of three steps to writing in this book each day. Writing and doing What's Your Dream Morning Routine every day for twenty-one days in a row, can develop a new way of seeing yourself as a person. My high school coach used to say to get strong at something, you needed to do it three times in a row. Doing WYDMR for twenty-one days three times in a row (yes sixty-three days) will create strength in doing a morning routine.

This book is designed to be an outline to invest love, joy, compassion, content and gratitude into who you are as a person. As we do this we become the person who creates and manifest our own dreams By writing about "what you love about other people," is writing about ways of "being" that you love. This awareness will support your development of the characteristics that you love and respect.

For example, I love people who decide to create an active healthy life that also supports and benefits other people. This way of living inspires me to invest more time around people I admire and respect.

. Here are a few more examples of "What do I love about other people? _____ Why? _____ "

Here are some examples of writing "What I love about others and why":
- I love people who run outside because I also love to run outside and seeing people run inspires me to run.
- I love relating and connecting with people because this challenges my self growth and learning.
- I love people who teach because I love to learn and learning from other people makes learning easier.
- I love people for sharing health and wellness because being healthy makes snowboarding, running,

mountain biking, and other outdoor activities more fun.
- I love people for sharing the benefits of focus because this supports creating excellence and I appreciate excellence and quality and the inspiration to practice focus by seeing what it has done for other people.
- I love people who spend allot of time outdoors because spending time outdoors is something I enjoy and appreciate and these people who remind me of this.

7

Write: What I Am Grateful For and Why?
(one to three minutes)

What Are My Favorite Natural Talents & Abilities?

What should we really be grateful for? Should we be grateful for our most basic needs for survival like food, shelter, clothing, family, friends? A common suggestion is to be grateful for what you have. Well, what do we really have? What if all we have is what we take with us when we die? Is it possible that when we die, things like innate goodness, joy, love, compassion, are what we leave this life with? If this is possible, what would it be like to be grateful for our favorite qualities, like love and compassion?

What is it about you that most inspires you? What quality or way of being, within yourself, are you grateful for? What qualities within other people are you're grateful to have learned about? What kind of actions, or ways of "being," have people shared with you that you're grateful for? What kind of person do you dream of being, and can you be grateful for this dream?

"Be grateful for your gifts."
—HH The Dalai Lama

"Gratitude is appreciating what you can do, and doing it!"
—MWW

Personalize your gratitude of your favorite qualities you possess by appreciating the qualities in yourself that are enjoyable to share. Try asking yourself which of the mental, emotional, spiritual, or physical gifts you're living, that you are grateful for. When writing about what you are grateful for think of the qualities you possess that support the experiences you enjoy. What qualities in others do you admire? How are you similar? In his 1983 book, Howard Gardner, *Frames of Mind: The Theory of Multiple Intelligences*, Basic Books; 3 edition (March 29, 2011), Howard Gardner writes about multiple types of intelligence —musical-rhythmic and harmonic, visual-spatial, verbal-linguistic, logical-mathematical, bodily-kinesthetic, intrapersonal, interpersonal, naturalistic, and existential.

Musical is sensitivity to sounds, rhythms, tones, and music. Visual is spacial judgement and the ability to visualize with the mind's eye. Verbal is a facility with words and languages. Logical is reasoning, numbers, critical thinking, underlying principles. Bodily-kinesthetic is control of one's bodily motions and the capacity to handle objects skillfully. Interpersonal is sensitivity to others moods, feelings temperaments, motivations, and ability to cooperate in a group. Intrapersonal is introspective and self-reflective capacities, understanding one-self. Naturalistic is ability to recognize animal and plant species, rocks, mountain types, oceans, for hunting, farming, biological science. IQ. (Wikipedia)

What gifts do you have? What do you appreciate about your gifts? This is what you'll get to write about for twenty-one days while doing WYDMR. If you are not clear on what gifts you may have or would like to get more specific into your gifts, strengths and personality, there are some books for studying these aspects of yourself listed below. The difference in what this morning routine offers and the books mentioned below is; this morning routine is a way to invest love, joy, compassion and content into your strengths, personality, natural intelligence and what you love about yourself. For example natural intelligence that I am gifted with includes music and nature. And one of the things I love is riding a bike. These are things I can appreciate about myself and use to write about during the 21-day What's Your Dream? Morning Routine (WYDMR). If you would like to go into learning about your strengths, natural intelligence, and/or personality before starting this morning routine, here are four books I would recommend looking into:

1. *Multiple Intelligences*, Howard Gardner, Copyright 2006 by Howard Gardner, First edition 1993 by Howard Gardner, Published by Basic Books A Member of Perseus Books Group.
2. *Now Discover Your Strengths,* Marcus Buckingham & Donald O. Clifton, THE FREE PRESS A Division of Simon & Schuster Inc. 1230 Avenue of the Americas New York, NY 10020
3. *THE ENNEAGRAM MADE EASY: Discover the 9 types of people.* Copyright 1994 By Renee Baron and Elizabeth Wagele. All right reserved. Harper Collins Publishers, 10 East 53rd Street, New York, NY 10022
4. *The Modern Enneagram: Discover Who You Are and Who You Can Be,* By Kacie Berghoef & Melanie Bell,

Althea Press 918 Parker Street, Suit A-12, Berkeley, CA 94710

These four books will give a person a more in-depth look at yourself and characteristics of yourself. Then during this WYDMR you can write what you love, enjoy, are compassionate with, content with, and grateful for. These books are not necessary to do this 21-day routine. A person can write and appreciate things like I have written about my enjoyment of bike riding and bike riding with people. However a person may get more out of doing this 21-day routine with more in-depth self study from these books mentioned above to practice self-love in a more in-depth way.

This next look at gratitude comes from the view that our suffering is an opportunity rather than a burden. What would we do with our lives if there were no such thing as the relief of suffering? Ever notice when the conflict or competition in a movie is over, so is the movie? One thing about suffering is that it's an opportunity to know ourselves and our unlimited ability to relieve suffering. Through this experience we become grateful for our suffering.

If we apply Gregg Braden's advice —"bless the things that hurt you" (WR 10) —and bless our own personality when it becomes angry, afraid, lonely, confused, jealous, or wanting something, we are creating a practice of self-compassion to relieve the causes of our suffering. When we bless the things in our personality that create our suffering, we can learn to stop causing our own suffering. We discover we are the relief to our own suffering. For example, if a person says something hurtful to me, rather than saying, "That person is being hurtful," I can say, "My anger toward this person is hurtful." Then I can bless my belief in being angry or the part of my personality that becomes angry at people who say things I don't like. And by taking responsibility for creating my own suffering, I am also taking the responsibility to relieve my suffering by being compassionate with my feelings, thoughts and beliefs. Another example is saying, "I bless the belief — living in "fear" is safer than living in "love."

When we go through difficult times, we have not learned our lesson until we find something about the difficult times that helped us learn something we like about ourselves. Feeling appreciation and gratitude for difficult times, comes from learning how to manage ourself in a way that creates happiness for ourselves and the people around us. As these skills develop we will also develop confidence to get through both difficult and good times; this creates the self-image and feeling of being a more complete person or feeling more whole and self-confident.

We can also bless the causes of our happiness. Like blessing the attributes we like about ourself is another example of practicing gratitude of who we are. "I bless my favorite attributes, innate intelligence, natural strengths, with love, compassion, joy and contentment." Blessing something is another way to practice gratitude.

Here are some examples of practicing gratitude. Examples of "Right now I am grateful for _____, because (or why)_____." (Be sure to speak out loud as you write.)

- Right now I am grateful for investing in my intention to be "more loving to myself and others," because this focus supports connecting with people and connecting with people is my greatest source of happiness.
- Right now I am grateful for forgiving myself for creating anger because being angry is painful, and forgiving myself is recognizing I don't want to suffer and being self compassionate.
- I bless my love of stillness and content because this makes it easier to focus on doing things I like to do.
- I bless calm people, because calm people go through life with ease and this inspires me to invest in being calm.
- I am grateful for my love of nature because I love nature and can learn more about life from nature.
- I bless my love of relating with people because a common love shared between myself and another is one of my favorite ways to create a friendship.

- I am grateful for my injury because learning how to heal myself is healthy and supports happiness.
- I'm grateful for athletic abilities because being active is fun. I appreciate being active—snowboarding, skiing, biking, running, and being outdoors with others who also enjoy these activities.
- I'm grateful for my love of learning because this has brought me to meet many highly gifted experts that have supported my learning.

8

Whom and How I Will Serve Today and Why?
Or, How Can I Share Appreciation of People Today?
(one to three minutes.)

If you're not making someone's life better, you're wasting your time.
—*Will Smith's Grandma* (WR 11)

One day in 2011, while working as a snowboard instructor, I was teaching a seven-year-old boy who was snowboarding for the first time. He was already an accomplished skier and could ski anywhere on the mountain. I noticed when he would fall, even a very simple fall that was nearly just sitting down in the snow, he would become upset. Then, while standing on his toes and facing

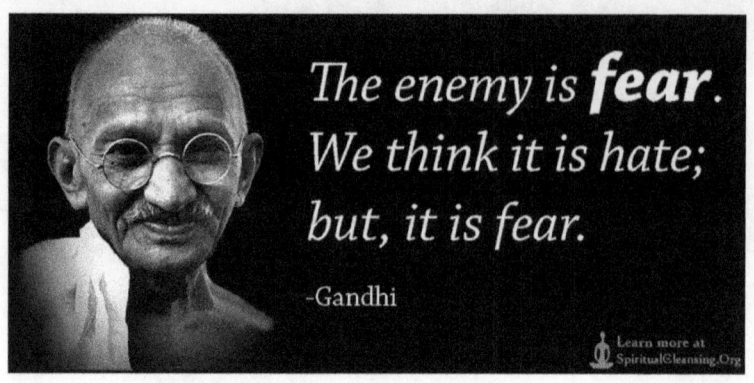

uphill, he slipped and went down onto his knees and started to cry. I asked the boy if he was hurt, and he said no. So I asked him why he was crying. He said he did not like falling. (He seemed to be putting a lot of pressure on himself to be able to snowboard with his friends without falling.) So I asked him why did he not want to fall? He said, "Because I don't like falling!" So I asked the boy, "What would snowboarding be like if falling was fun?" He sat there for a moment and said, "I don't like falling." "Okay." I said, and asked, "Just curious, though. What would snowboarding be like if falling was fun?" "What do you mean?" he asked. "I mean sometimes spinning, rolling, and tumbling can be fun." "Can you do a somersault?" I asked. He replied, "Not with a snowboard on." I said, "I can. Wanna see?" "Sure," he said. So I rolled forward with my snowboard on and did a somersault—sort of. The boy said, "That's not a somersault; that was a shoulder roll." "I wrestle with my dad every night, and I know the difference between a shoulder roll and a somersault," he said. I replied, "Okay, show me a somersault." He proceeded to do a somersault with his snowboard on—a nice, straight somersault without leaning to one side like I did. Then I asked, "That was really good. Can you do a shoulder roll also?" He said, "Easy!" and proceeded to do a shoulder roll. Then he said, "Now do a real somersault." So I did a real somersault onto my back not to the side on a shoulder. Then we did somersaults and shoulder rolls down the entire beginner hill. At the bottom of the hill we both stood up laughing. Then we went back up the hill and learned how to make snowboard turns. We never talked about falling again.

This boy was able to overcome his pain, anger, and fear through play. And after facing his fear, he became happy. My intention in teaching snowboarding is not to teach someone how to ride. My intention is to share with people my love of snowboarding and to support people in creating their own love of snowboarding.

This is similar to this book. I love my intention to create my dream of supporting people being more themselves as a way to create and manifest dreams. I am sharing this love by writing this book. And if this book inspires your intention to be more yourself to create and manifest your dreams, that's cool too. 😎

This step, serving and sharing what you love, brings the previous two steps together to create an intention for your day. There is no goal to create results here. The intention is to be proactively sharing and serving people in a way you love and enjoy.

One of the qualities of happiness is that happiness is a result of our actions. This step is to create the intention to be loving, joyful, compassionate and/or content with your actions for the day. Then, at the end of the day, notice your mood with openness to both a positive or negative mood. What gets rewarded gets repeated, so noticing a positive mood can help support the actions that created this positive mood. If at the end of the day your mood seems negative try looking at the energy put into your intention. For example; if our intention is to be loving with our actions at work, and at the end of the day we are in a bad mood, then it is possible our energy related to our intention is negative or based in fear rather than love. If this happens being open to the question, "What if I don't know what love is?" can change our life. By practicing loving ourself everyday and noticing our interactions with other people and our effect on people, we can start to create energy that we enjoy sharing and people who we interact with also enjoy.

Pretend you're in an ocean of what we call consciousness. Notice your awareness of taste, touch, smell, sight, hearing, thinking, and feeling. Now notice yourself trying, wanting, and desiring to be happy, independent, inspired, a friend, wealthy, smart, strong, beautiful, natural, healthy, successful, helpful, supportive, brave, a superhero, an explorer, a scientist, an actor, a writer, etc. If there is a way of "being" we want to experience, why are we not experiencing such a thing right now, in this moment? Could it be we're afraid of getting out of that ocean of who we think we are? What if this consciousness that we want to change or be different, is like being in slightly cold water and we want to get out, yet we fear we will get even colder when we get out? Could this be the "fear" Gandhi is speaking of? It has been said that all suffering comes from desire, or all suffering comes from thought. Allen Watts says, (VR 10) "We suffer because we enjoy it." Well, what fish does not enjoy swimming?

Thus, if we are living in an ocean of desire or thoughts that are causing our suffering, trying to get out of this consciousness is like a fish trying to get out of water. Does the fish notice the water? Can we notice our state of "being?" Can we see ourselves as a fish looking out of the ocean onto dry land and seeing land animals? Would we then want to walk on dry land like the land animals? Would this awareness of land animals and wanting to walk on land help us see we are breathing water? To make this metaphor more real, would noticing very happy people inspire a person to invest more energy into being happy? Even at the risk of losing an identity of unhappiness? This may sound crazy, but what if this meant giving up all the love coming from all the people who know you as being unhappy?

If we learn to serve people, coming from a place of what we love and what we are grateful for, could this action be seen as crawling out of an old way of "being"? Would sharing what a person loves and is grateful for, support manifesting your dreams? This book is written with this belief.

What if we we look at our personality as the world we live in? This question helped me notice that how we treat and create our personality. Have you ever thought about how you treat yourself or your personality? If we became more purposeful in how treat and create our personality, would this have a ripple effect on our life? Could these ideas help support an inspiration of doing a morning routine that includes self-care?

Why serve each other? Let's look at what this book is about—*creating and manifesting your dreams*. So let's ask this question, can we be happy without serving other people?

Noticing how we treat ourselves and other people is the answer to becoming a happier person.

—*MWW*

As I wrote this book and practiced noticing my thought process, I also noticed thoughts of things getting worse. The thoughts of things getting worse included my relationships, my living situation, my finances, my health, and more. When these types of thoughts are at the back of our mind and not noticed, they happen as if they are just life. Have you ever heard someone say, "Life happens"? Would "I'm happening to myself again" be more true? What kind of intention lies behind statements like "Life happens"? When we make an intention to create and manifest our dreams to be happy, we start to notice the way we think of ourselves. This awareness supports becoming a happier person by being more aware of our own thoughts, actions, and intentions with ourselves and others.

"To live in service to humanity, to live in service to your family, to your church, to your city, to your country, to the world, that is the purest form of joy."
—Will Smith

So let's make serving fun. In step one —"What I love about myself and other people"—we look at qualities about ourselves and others that we love. In step two, we look at what we are grateful for, as in qualities or ways of "being" within ourselves. And now we create the intention to share what we love and what we are grateful for with other people today. This is how we manifest our dreams, by sharing what we love we are fulfilling are dream of how we would like to be as a person. Our dreams do not manifest as a result of serving people. Our dreams manifest when we love and enjoy what and how we are serving people. Find what you love in your personality, strengths and natural intelligence, and apply this morning routine exercise of being loving, joyful, compassionate and content with these qualities of yourself. This practice will be your guiding light to find and do what you would love to share with the world. Do what you love by practicing gratitude for what you appreciate about yourself and others. And share what you love as a way to serve others.

A note on writing about service to others: write about and serve people without dependence on any outcome. Serve with an intention of being open to any outcome and *noticing if you like what and how you're sharing.* For example, we might focus on serving people with intention to accept each person just as they are. We could focus on serving people with respect from our experience of practicing self-respect. What quality about yourself do you enjoy? Can you share it? Is there a reason why you like to share or serve with this quality? Personally, I like sharing appreciation for the time and energy put into creating toys because I love to play with toys and because playing supports fun interactions and connections with people.

Here are some examples of intention to serve people:

- Today I am serving people with the love of being creative with words because I love connecting with people through a mutual understanding created with words.
- Today I am serving people who love health and fitness by investing in my health and sharing appreciation of people who also love and invest in health.
- Today I am serving people with my love of learning by supporting and being a benefit any way I can for people whom I interact with that are also investing in learning.
- Today I am serving and benefiting people who love biking by being very aware of and safely driving around bikers.
- Today I am serving people with my love of being successful by sharing appreciation for everyone I interact with during the day because my success only comes with the support of other people.

How can your intention to serve support your community involvement?

Would writing an intention of serving people by sharing something about yourself that you love, create more awareness of how and why you are contributing to society?

9

Ask "What Would It Take? to Create Intention

This last exercise is to practice intention by asking, "What would it take?" In this step we are not trying to answer the question, we ask the question to create the intention to experience an answer. Often when we are asked or ask ourself a question we are then trying to find an answer to a question. With this practice of intention it is more important to invest love, joy, compassion and content into our question, "What would it take to experience, be, create (fill in the blank)? This will support finding or creating an answer we enjoy.

How Can Loving a Characteristic of Myself Lead My Life into My Dreams?

Creating and supporting our dreams with positive loving, compassionate, joy, equanimity and content is key to creating and manifesting our dreams. Our dreams are grown from the ground we plant them in. If we are living in fear, jealousy, anger, pride, loneliness, shame, blame or a low energy that we have gotten used to living in. For example there was a time when I was trying to manifest living in a four bedroom, five bathroom, three car garage home in the mountains. At the time I was very lonely, fearful of my financial situation, and angrily trying to prove to people I can manifest my dreams. Then I found this house and rented a bedroom for only $700 a month and moved in. The landlord then rented out two of the other rooms and within six months one of my roommates physically threatened me and I moved out. This experience then supported me living in fear of trying to manifest my dreams. Going into this fear with compassion has supported me developing this 21-day routine that exercises our love, joy, compassion and content of our favorite strengths, personality traits, natural intelligence, and things about ourself we love and enjoy. This 21-day routine works because the more positive energy of love, joy, compassion and content we shine on our own innate way of being, the more we are being ourself. Just like a hunting dog will point out where the birds are hiding and a rescue dog will find people who are hidden under snow, these dogs both have similar yet different innate talents just like we do. This book will support and develop your own natural talents from the daily exercises of applying love, joy, compassion and equanimity to these talents. The daily exercises of applying these positive energies into your talents will also support and grow your gratitude of these talents and awareness of positive growth of yourself. As this growth takes place and we become more ourself with this positive energy, we will also naturally be investing positive energy into developing and manifesting our dreams. The reason why this works is because if we are a logical person then logic is something we already love. As we create more awareness of how we love our logical personality we are exercising our positive expression of love (or joy, compassion, content.)

I have found that to be more of ourselves just knowing what are natural talents and personality is and doing cognitive exercises and studying these traits will not develop our greatest and most important talents of love, joy, compassion and equanimity or content. Because **applying our positive energy to ourself, our lives and the people around us is what will guide us into creating and manifesting our dreams.**

So another exercise of applying our positive energy of will now be applied to the question "What would it take?" We will be adding four magic words that make our intention positive and a benefit for us and others. These four magic words come from a practice of kindness Sharon Salzberg who shared this in the CD she coauthors with Nawang Khechog, *A Cup of Kindness*. (RP 2) These magic words are *safe*, *happy*, *healthy*, and *with ease*. We can use these words to enhance our intention created with the question "What would it take?" By adding these four statements, we are creating an answer that will benefit us and others, and add enjoyment to creating our intention.

When we add the word *safely* to "What would it take?" we are creating intention to do no harm. This supports our intention to create happiness because it is a wish to prevent suffering. When our intention does not cause harm, the experience of our intention can be enjoyed even more. This question to create our intention is now "What would it take to safely _____?"

When we add *happily* to "What would it take?" we are adding the wish to be happy while experiencing our intention. For example, if a person intends to go for a bike ride and during the bike ride this person gets upset because of a flat tire or rain, this person did not enjoy their intention of going for a bike ride. If we include happiness in our intention, then taking a break from riding to fix a flat or being cooled off by the rain is less likely to upset a person. Adding *happily* to our intention can take pressure off creating a specific experience and put more value into our way of being. This question to create our intention is now "What would it take to happily _____?"

By adding *healthfully* to "What would it take?" is adding a future benefit to our experience. For example, when we do something healthy, like eating organic fruits and vegetables, exercising, sleeping well, or make other investments in our health, we are creating a future benefit for ourselves. Doing things in a healthy way creates a future benefit. This question to create our intention is now "What would it take to healthfully_____?"

By adding *easily* to "What would it take?" we are creating the intention for what we want to experience to be stress free—to do so without effort or strain. Doing things with ease can also create self-confidence. Making things important, urgent, life-changing, or critical can put unnecessary stress on a situation. This last wish is to create an intention to experience your intention with ease. For example, this question becomes "How can I easily_____?"

This question is part of this daily routine. It is to create the intention to experience what you would like to experience. Remember, this step is only asking a question and not trying to answer it. By asking questions we activate intention. Trying to answer the question can get in the way of allowing intention to manifest. The daily question, then, is **"What would it take to safely, happily, healthfully, and easily—experience, do, share, be?"**

Examples of filling in the blank are "feel more at peace," "be more self-confident," "create a relationship," "go to college," "create a business," "experience less trying and wanting," "experience more doing," "benefit more people with sharing what I love," or "learn something new." We can ask for whatever we want.

And if it doesn't show up right away, as Jim Carry says, "It's because the universe is busy filling my request." (VR7)

"Let it go" is KEY! This phrase can be a common saying without real meaning. To add some meaning to it, I have had some help from Gregg Braden. Gregg has told a story a number of times on YouTube about a friend of his who took Gregg to a sacred place to pray for rain during a severe drought in New Mexico. Gregg said that his friend, with his back to Gregg, put his hands in the prayer position against his chest, made an offering, then turned to Gregg and asked him if he would like to get something to eat. (VR8)

This has helped me manifest and create dreams coming true in knowing that what we are dreaming and praying for is an offering to the universe. This is very important, so let me say it again: our dreams and prayers are offerings of what we would like to share with this world. With this in mind, we can more naturally let go of our dreams and prayers. This is a way of thinking that can change our point of view from wanting to offering, from getting and having to sharing and being. When we think our dreams as just for ourselves, this is when we hold on to them. It is our happiness we long to share, and offering our dreams and prayers is a way to do this. Think of your prayers of health, wealth, relationships, and happiness as an offering to the universe. And be generous.

Gregg Braden also suggests touching the center of our chest while making an offering. (VR 8) This touch will direct our attention to this area of our body—our heart. Our heart produces the most electrical and magnetic energy of any part of our body, even many times more than our brain. The idea is to focus energy toward our prayers and intention. A light touch of the finger or thumb side of our hand over the heart brings awareness to this area. This brings more energy to our prayers, wishes, and intention.

10

Reward Yourself for Doing WYD?MR
Cultivate a Warm Heart for Doing WYD?MR!!

As I was writing this book and creating WYDMR there seemed to be breakthroughs where I said, "This is it! This will make this book GREAT!" Then after working on a new step to WYDMR, it still felt like something was missing. The difference in this step from the other parts of WYDMR is that cultivating a warm heart is not a cognitive or thinking part of WYDMR. In this step we practice self love and care of ourself, for creating awareness of what we love, what we are grateful for, and how we will serve people today. This last step of WYDMR is **appreciation of taking fifteen to twenty minutes to value oneself as a person**. This is the reward each time a person does WYD?MR. This is the cherry on top, icing on the cake, the hug from a loved one just for being you. In this step we cultivate a warm heart for ourself and for taking the time to appreciate and love ourself.

What is a warm heart? Hear is a story to help define a warm heart. In 2013 I was at a convention or gathering of people and a person was at the podium in the room getting ready to make a presentation to about fifty people in the room. The person at the podium was talking to herself going over the parts of the presentation. Her voice was echoing in the room. Suddenly she said, "Oh my gosh I'm taking to myself with the microphone on." And she started laughing out loud, with a happy and gentle laughter. This laughter filled the room with a warmth that ignited the room with more laughter.

From this experience my definition or sign of a warm heart is a person's ability to warmly, lovingly, and in a caring way—laugh at oneself. And that is this step in WYDMR. Cultivating a warm heart creates happiness and being happy is the key to making our dreams come true. This is my favorite step in WYDMR, and the key to making this step work is doing all the other parts of WYDMR honestly and with determination.

In this step we go back to the questions we have answered and written out and do more than read them out loud. While we read our answers out loud we touch our hand or finger to the middle of our chest just left of our heart.

This is Greg Braden tip as mentioned earlier. This is to bring awareness to our heart so we are not just thinking we are being caring.

Then after reading what we have written for the day we laugh warmly and lovingly for noticing we have completed WYDMR for the day.

The key to laughing at completing WYDMR is to to be laughing with enjoyment of ourself. This step is expressing enjoyment of what we love about ourself. For example I may laugh with myself for loving bike riding. This is a positive expression of loving myself for enjoying bike riding. Laughing abut what we love expresses our enjoyment of what we love and can support a positive self image of who we like to be and how we like to share ourselves with the world. I love myself for being athletic, Ha Ha! I love myself for being a writer, Ha Ha! I love myself for creating awareness of what I love, what I am grateful for, and how I am going to serve people today, Ha Ha Ha!

The more I express enjoyment of what I love with laughter the more I find myself doing things I love. Have you ever heard someone say, "I need to go to the gym and work out because I have not gone in a while." This statement does not express a person's enjoyment of exercising, a need is not an enjoyment. Creating more awareness of what we enjoy about what we are doing, will support a self-image of being a person who enjoys life. Sometimes when I talk about people who inspire me—people who are very good at what they do, someone might express a dislike to a person's mastery of a skill. This dislike is an example of our fear and/or dislike of "greatness." The more a person spends time appreciating what they love, the more a person may gravitate towards becoming proficient at doing what they love. This may separate a person from being average to being an expert or developing mastery at doing what a person loves. For example some of the things I love include telemark skiing and snowboarding. And the practices in this book of creating awareness of what I love have supported and inspired me to snowboard and telemark ski. For the last eight years I have averaged over 100 days a season skiing and snowboarding. This means my life includes playing an average of twenty days a month in the winter season. This is an example of how a daily routine can create a person's experiences or create dreams coming true.

"*My style of fighting is not fighting.*"

—*Bruce Lee* (VR 9)

The important part to notice about this step is that here in the U.S our culture for a long time has been fed the idea of being against things. Being against cancer, obesity, poverty, people put in prison for doing the wrong thing. ("Though only five percent of the world's population lives in the United States, it is home to 25% of the world's prison population." Washington Post April 30, 2015)

This book and this step in WYDMR in particular, is about *being for* your health, wealth, and relationships. Instead of being against cancer, obesity, poverty, or other illnesses. This book is about supporting the love of being healthy, wealthy and having close relationships. Being healthy means a person does not have illness to fight against. Being wealthy means a person does not live in poverty and therefore is not fighting against their own poverty. And most importantly a person who invest in their own love, joy, compassion and peace with a warm heart, will naturally develop healthy relationships.

What's Your Dream Morning Routine will support you to craft and cultivate your own greatness and unlimited potential by developing a greater sense of awareness and appreciation of what you love with laughter. And the reason we laugh is because being great at what we love is enjoyable. What is important is how we treat ourselves and the people we love.

The End of WYDMR—Let the River Flow

Let Go of Control —Love Is a Way of Being, Not a Goal.

"Being at ease with not knowing is crucial for answers to come to you."

—Eckhart Tolle (BR 6)

Once you've finished your daily WYDMR exercises, your intention is set, so let it go. Our world is largely made up of trying or working for something in the future. For example, we try to be happy, educated, thin, wealthy, healthy, and safe by working to achieve these things. Trying to be something in the future is a form of suffering because happiness is only in the present. When we are trying to accomplish something for future happiness, we are not being happy in the moment. And the more focused we become on the moment, the better we perform in the moment. This is acting with intention. This can be seen in athletes, writers, scientists, martial arts, yoga,

and artists as being present at a heightened state of awareness. It's also called "the zone" or "getting in the flow."

Happiness is experiencing your true self or "selflessness." Some people say we (people) and everything in the universe are energy. Energy is a very small part of what we are. For example, "a hydrogen atom is about 99.9999999999996 percent empty space" (Google). Put another way, the energy in a hydrogen atom takes up about 0.000000000004 percent of the space of the atom.

The energy of the atom is an extremely small part of the complete volume of an atom. The space within the atom is the largest part of the atom. Similarly, it is said that thoughts and feelings are energy. What if the energy of thoughts and feelings is a very tiny part of who we are? If this were true, would it mean being selfless (being free of our thoughts and emotions) would help us see our true self? Being "selfless" has been described by artists, athletes, writers, scientists, spiritual leaders, and others as a high state of awareness, or mindfulness. Is recognizing our true self the recognition of being "space" as an experience? You may be asking, "How can the recognition of space be related to happiness?" To cut to the chase, the answer is that space is unlimited potential. The recognition of oneself as space is the recognition of one's own unlimited potential.

This is what I believe this Zen drawing represents: space, emptiness, and unlimited potential. We are creating the experience of selflessness. We can create this experience by serving others, participating in group collaboration toward a common  goal, meditation, intense mindfulness, intense pain or depression, intense happiness, and in life-challenging activities where extreme athletes describe themselves as having a very high and expanded sense of awareness. However, the experience of selflessness is created, and the experience of selflessness has been described as happiness by people who have described having such an experience.

    The rest of the book is the exercises and outline for your to create and manifest your dreams with intention by finding, doing, and sharing what you love. Noticing the happiness that comes from this is the reward. And what gets rewarded gets repeated. Notice and appreciate yourself creating and manifesting your dreams.

Letting Go of Homelessness

Dose WYDMR really create dreams coming true, and can it make your life better? It has for me. On October 26, 2016, I got a job in the Aspen Valley that included housing. This was a really nice day when I was able to move back into an apartment with a new appreciation for shelter. This new appreciation includes many people not mentioned at

the beginning of this book, including employers because this supported paying for expenses like car insurance, my phone, and a gym membership that provided a place for exercising and a shower. I'm also grateful to those who've shared laughter, because it makes life so enjoyable. I've also gained a new appreciation for being able to *simply relax*. One of the things about being homeless and living in a car for the summer is that it takes a lot of energy—energy to not sleep, energy to work, energy of finding a better paying job and trying to find a way to get back into housing, and energy to write this book.

Now I'm also finding motivation to keep improving my lifestyle by doing WYDMR. This has developed my understanding that an improved lifestyle comes from happiness. I'm continuously inspired to create, manifest and share my dreams. Sometimes this is hard when I am looking for a way to support myself "now." Accepting the "now" sometimes seems like a compromise to what I want. Yet what I have learned from writing and creating this book is that it's not our "dream coming true" that we want. What we really want is to treat ourself as a person who can create and manifest our dreams to share with the world. And **as we create more awareness and intention in how we treat ourself we become the person who manifest dreams and shares them for the benefit of other people.**

Now that I'm living in Aspen, playing with ways to be happy includes working on my skills of skateboarding, snowboarding, skiing, running, writing, selling books, driving, teaching, and learning about opportunities in business and life. Also noticing how I am "being." And enjoying my new understanding and appreciation of the importance of how I am treating myself and others. Thanks to everyone I know for being in my life. *Life only gets better with gratitude.* What will WYDMR do for you?

If I was ten-times happier, If I was one-hundred times happier, what would I be doing, what would my dreams be for myself?

Think of yourself as a radiating light of health wealth and happiness that brightens everything and everyone around you. See yourself as a bright healing light who creates healing in the earth, plants and nature by walking the earth. See yourself as a healing light that heals people within one hundred yards of you. People are relieved of all physical, mental and spiritual ailments from being in your presence. Than answer this question, "What would I be doing, what would my dreams be for myself?—with the state of mind of being one-hundred times happier. Answer this question with your lifetime in mind. What experiences in life would you invest in creating—such things as spirituality, art, science, communication, nature, social, family, health (mental, physical, emotional), or general well-being —in your life. Simply focus on how you would be inspired to live as a person that is one-hundred times happier than you are right now.

(Here is some space to write your answers.)

What part of my innate goodness; love, joy, compassion and peace, would I like to expand my understanding of, to support my dreams coming true?

If a person's dream is to create happiness by doing art, the next question is, "How can I express love, joy, compassion or equanimity to create art?" This question becomes a very individual question. In what way would you like to express yourself in your art? (We can also replace art with, science, logic, communication, a personality trait like helper, perfectionist, or strength like learner, creative, or something we like to do like bike riding or playing.)

Here are some descriptions of love, joy, compassion and peace. Please use you own definition if these don't help you answer the question.
- Love: The wish for all beings to be happy.
- Joy: "When the mind is pure, joy follows like a shadow that never leaves." Gautama Buddha,
- Compassion: The wish for all beings to be free from suffering.
- Content: The freedom of allowing everyone and everything to be just as it is.

Which one of the four thoughts; love, joy, compassion, or peace, would you enjoy expressing while doing what you love to do?

(Here is some space to write your answer on the following two pages.)

What does; what you want to do, how you want to be (loving, joyful, compassionate, or at peace), and what you share with world, have to do with your connections with other people?

In my experience with creating and manifesting dreams, the single most important factor is our relationships with other people. Whether friends, family, or significant others, our relationships are the biggest determining factor in achieving happiness. In the movie "Ip Man III," Ip Man has a fight with another master martial artist. It's a great battle that Ip Man wins in the end. The other fighter becomes very upset at his loss and smashes a beautiful wooden carved sign that proclaimed him as a grand master. Ip Man says to his opponent, "What's important is how we treat the people we are close to." I think of this metaphor whenever I am investing in creating a dream. Because whatever our label is at this time; janitor, politician, cook, doctor, teacher, student, rich, poor, any way we see ourself, what is important is how we are treating ourselves and others. This journaling book is designed to support a person create greater awareness and intention of how we are treating ourselves and others. Answer the three questions above and notice what your answers have to do with social connections.

In what ways do the answers to these three questions support more meaningful and new relationships for you? Here is some space to write your answers.

What's Your Dream Morning Routine

Congratulations on starting a morning routine to create and manifest your dreams!

Along with answering these questions every day for twenty-one days, follow the outline of WYDMR on page 27, which includes drinking water, slow breathing and smiling for three minutes, self-care, and self-commitment. Answering these questions each day along with the exercises listed on page 27 is what makes up WYDMR.

Note: Using two bookmarks, one for WYDMR outline (page 28) and one for the page a day (day 1–21 of WYDMR) will help keep you organized when doing WYDMR.

Day 1 Date: _____

- What I love about Myself & Others, and Why? (Write for 1–3 minutes)

Day 1
- I am grateful for (personal characteristic), and Why? (write for 1-3 minutes)

Day 1

- Whom and how will I serve today, and why?

(Write for 1–3 minutes)

Day 1

- What would it take to safely, happily, healthfully, and easily; experience, do, share, or be? (Write 1-3 minutes)

- In ten words or less write what you are noticing about yourself from doing these writing exercises.

- Now touch your hand to the left side of your sternum over your heart and read out loud what you wrote this morning. Do this while laughing out loud to cultivate a warm heart for investing in being more yourself.

Day 2 Date: _____

- What I Love About Myself & Others, and Why? (Write for 1–3 minutes)

Day 2

- I am grateful for (personal characteristics), and Why? (Write for 1–3 minutes)

Day 2

- Whom and how will I serve today, and why?
(Write for 1–3 minutes)

Day 2

- What would it take to safely, happily, healthfully, and easily; experience, do, share, or be? (Write 1-3 minutes)

- In ten words or less write what you are noticing about yourself from doing these writing exercises.

- Now touch your hand to the left side of your sternum over your heart and read out loud what you wrote this morning. Do this while laughing out loud to cultivate a warm heart for investing in being more yourself.

Day 3 Date: _____

- What I Love About Myself & Others, and Why? (Write for 1–3 minutes.)

Day 3

- I am grateful for (personal characteristics), and why? (Write for 1–3 minutes.)

Day 3

- Whom and how will I serve today, and why? (Write for 1–3 minutes.)

Day 3

- What would it take to safely, happily, healthfully, and easily; experience, do, share, be? (Write 1-3 minutes)

- In ten words or less write what you are noticing about yourself from doing these writing exercises.

- Now touch your hand to the left side of your sternum over your heart and read out loud what you wrote this morning. Do this while laughing out loud to cultivate a warm heart for investing in being more yourself.

3 days into creating a self-image of a dream creator! Make it play!

Day 4 Date: _____

- What I Love About Myself & Others, and Why? (Write for 1–3 minutes.)

Day 4
- I am grateful for (personal characteristics), and Why? (Write for 1–3 minutes.)

Day 4

- Whom and how will I will serve today, and why? (Write for 1–3 minutes.)

Day 4

- What would it take to safely, happily, healthfully, and easily; experience, do, share, be? (Write 1-3 minutes)

- In ten words or less write what you are noticing about yourself from doing these writing exercises.

- Now touch your hand to the left side of your sternum over your heart and read out loud what you wrote this morning. Do this while laughing out loud to cultivate a warm heart for investing in being more yourself.

Day 5 Date: _____

• What I Love About Myself & Others, and Why? (Write for 1–3 minutes.)

Day 5

- I am grateful for (personal characteristics), and Why? (Write for 1–3 minutes.)

Day 5

- Whom and how I will serve today? and Why? (Write for 1–3.)

Day 5

- What would it take to safely, happily, healthfully, and easily; experience, do, share, be? (Write for 1-3 minutes.)

- In ten words or less write what you are noticing about yourself from doing these writing exercises.

- Now touch your hand to the left side of your sternum over your heart and read out loud what you wrote this morning. Do this while laughing out loud to cultivate a warm heart for investing in being more yourself.

Day 6 Date: _____

- What I love about Myself & Others, and Why? (Write for 1–3 minutes.)

Day 6
- I am grateful for (personal characteristics) and Why? (Write for 1–3 minutes.)

Day 6

- Whom and how I will serve today, and Why? (Write for 1–3 minutes.)

Day 6

- What would it take to safely, happily, healthfully, and easily; experience, do, share, be? (Write 1-3 minutes)

- In ten words or less write what you are noticing about yourself from doing these writing exercises.

- Now touch your hand to the left side of your sternum over your heart and read out loud what you wrote this morning. Do this while laughing out loud to cultivate a warm heart for investing in being more yourself.

Day 7 Date: _____

• What I Love About Myself & Others, and Why? (Write for 1–3 minutes.)

Day 7
- I am grateful for (personal characteristics) and why? (Write for 1–3 minutes.)

Day 7

- Whom and how I will will serve today, and why? (Write for 1–3 minutes.)

Day 7

- What would it take to happily, healthfully, and easily; experience, do, share, be? (Write for 1-3 minutes.)

- In ten words or less write what you are noticing about yourself from doing these writing exercises.

- Now touch your hand to the left side of your sternum over your heart and read out loud what you wrote this morning. Do this while laughing out loud to cultivate a warm heart for investing in being more yourself.

Congratulations! You're 1/3 of the way to living a new self-image created with love, joy, compassion & content!!

Day 8 Date: _____

• What I Love About Myself & Others, and Why? (Write for 1–3 minutes.)

Day 8

- I am grateful for (personal characteristics) and Why? (Write for 1–3 minutes.)

Day 8

- Whom and how I will serve today, and Why? (Write for 1–3 minutes.)

Day 8

- What would it take to safely, happily, healthfully, and easily; experience, do, share, be? (Write 1-3 minutes)

- In ten words or less write what you are noticing about yourself from doing these writing exercises.

- Now touch your hand to the left side of your sternum over your heart and read out loud what you wrote this morning. Do this while laughing out loud to cultivate a warm heart for investing in being more yourself.

Do something fun today, even if for only 3 minutes!

Day 9 Date: _____

- What I Love About Myself & Others, and Why? (Write for 1–3 minutes.)

Day 9

- I am grateful for (personal characteristics) and why? (Write for 1–3 minutes.)

Day 9

- Whom and how will I will serve today, and why? (Write for 1–3 minutes.)

Day 9

- What would it take to safely, happily, healthfully, and easily; experience, do, share, be? (Write 1-3 minutes.)

- In ten words or less write what you are noticing about yourself from doing these writing exercises.

- Now touch your hand to the left side of your sternum over your heart and read out loud what you wrote this morning. Do this while laughing out loud to cultivate a warm heart for investing in being more yourself.

Day 10 Date: _____

- What I Love About Myself & Others, and Why? (Write for 1–3 minutes.)

Day 10
- I am grateful for (personal characteristics), and why? (Write for 1–3 minutes.)

Day 10

- Whom and how will I serve today, and why? (Write for 1–3 minutes.)

Day 10

- What would it take to safely, happily, healthfully, and easily; experience, do, share, be? (Write 1-3 minutes.)

- In ten words or less write what you are noticing about yourself from doing these writing exercises.

- Now touch your hand to the left side of your sternum over your heart and read out loud what you wrote this morning. Do this while laughing out loud to cultivate a warm heart for investing in being more yourself.

Day 11 Date: _____

- What I Love About Myself & Others, and Why? (Write for 1–3 minutes.)

Day 11

- What I am grateful for (personal characteristics) and Why? (Write for 1–3 minutes.)

Day 11

- Whom and how I will serve today and why? _____ (Write for 1–3 minutes.)

Day 11

- What would it take to safely, happily, healthfully, and easily; experience, do, share, be? (Write 1-3 minutes)

- In ten words or less write what you are noticing about yourself from doing these writing exercises.

- Now touch your hand to the left side of your sternum over your heart and read out loud what you wrote this morning. Do this while laughing out loud to cultivate a warm heart for investing in being more yourself.

What has been the funnest part of doing this routine?

Day 12 Date: _____
- What I Love About Myself & Others, and Why? (Write for 1–3 minutes.)

Day 12

- What I am grateful for (personal characteristics), and why? (Write for 1–3 minutes.)

Day 12

- Whom and how I will serve today, and why? (Write for 1–3 minutes.)

Day 12

- What would it take to safely, happily, healthfully, and easily; experience, do, share, be? (Write 1-3 minutes)

- In ten words or less write what you are noticing about yourself from doing these writing exercises.

- Now touch your hand to the left side of your sternum over your heart and read out loud what you wrote this morning. Do this while laughing out loud to cultivate a warm heart for investing in being more yourself.

Day 13 Date: _____

- What I Love About Myself, Others, and Why? (Write for 1–3 minutes)

Day 13
- What I am grateful for (personal characteristics) and why? (Write for 1–3 minutes)

Day 13

- Whom and how I will serve today, and why? (Write for 1–3 minutes)

Day 13

- What would it take to safely, happily, healthfully, and easily; experience, do, share, be?

- In ten words or less write what you are noticing about yourself from doing these writing exercises.

- Now touch your hand to the left side of your sternum over your heart and read out loud what you wrote this morning. Do this while laughing out loud to cultivate a warm heart for investing in being more yourself.

Day 14 Date: _____
- What I Love About Myself & Others, and Why? (Write for 1–3 minutes.)

Day 14

- What I am grateful for (personal characteristics) and Why? (Write for 1–3 minutes.)

Day 14

- Whom and how I will serve today, and Why? (Write for 1–3 minutes.)

Day 14

- What would it take to safely, happily, healthfully, and easily; experience, do, share, be? (Write 1-3 minutes)

- In ten words or less write what you are noticing about yourself from doing these writing exercises.

- Now touch your hand to the left side of your sternum over your heart and read out loud what you wrote this morning. Do this while laughing out loud to cultivate a warm heart for investing in being more yourself.

Congratulations! You're 2/3 of the way to living and being your dream self-image!! Are you noticing yourself going into your dreams?

Day 15 Date: _____

- What I Love About Myself & Others, and Why? (Write for 1–3 minutes.)

Day 15

- What I am grateful for (personal characteristics) and Why? (Write for 1–3 minutes.)

Day 15

• Whom and how I will serve today, and why? (Write for 1–3 minutes.)

Day 15

- What would it take to safely, happily, healthfully, and easily; experience, do, share, be? (Write 1-3 minutes)

- In ten words or less write what you are noticing about yourself from doing these writing exercises.

- Now touch your hand to the left side of your sternum over your heart and read out loud what you wrote this morning. Do this while laughing out loud to cultivate a warm heart for investing in being more yourself.

Day 16 Date: _____

• What I Love About Myself & Others, and Why? (Write for 1–3 minutes.)

Day 16
- "What I am grateful for (personal characteristics) and why? (Write for 1–3 minutes.)

Are you noticing any difference in relationships or your communication with people?

Day 16

- Whom and how I will serve today and why? (Write for 1–3 minutes)

Day 16

- What would it take to safely, happily, healthfully, and easily; experience, do, share, be? (Write for 1–3 minutes.)

- In ten words or less write what you are noticing about yourself from doing these writing exercises.

- Now touch your hand to the left side of your sternum over your heart and read out loud what you wrote this morning. Do this while laughing out loud to cultivate a warm heart for investing in being more yourself.

Day 17 Date: _____

- What I Love About Myself & Others, and Why? (Write for 1–3 minutes.)

Day 17

- "What I am grateful for (personal characteristics) and Why? (Write for 1–3 minutes.)

Day 17

- Whom and how I will serve today, and why? (Write for 1–3 minutes.)

Day 17

- What would it take to safely, happily, healthfully, and easily; experience, do, share, be? (Write 1-3 minutes)

- In ten words or less write what you are noticing about yourself from doing these writing exercises.

- Now touch your hand to the left side of your sternum over your heart and read out loud what you wrote this morning. Do this while laughing out loud to cultivate a warm heart for investing in being more yourself.

Day 18 Date: _____

• What I Love About Myself & Others, and Why? (Write for 1–3 minutes.)

Day 18

- What I am grateful for (personal characteristics) and Why? (Write for 1–3 minutes.)

Day 18

- Whom and how I will serve today, and why? (Write for 1–3 minutes.)

Day 18

- What would it take to safely, happily, healthfully, and easily; experience, do, share, be? (Write 1-3 minutes)

- In ten words or less write what you are noticing about yourself from doing these writing exercises.

- Now touch your hand to the left side of your sternum over your heart and read out loud what you wrote this morning. Do this while laughing out loud to cultivate a warm heart for investing in being more yourself.

How is doing a morning routine to manifest your dreams affecting your life?

Day 19 Date: _____
- What I Love About Myself & Others, and Why? (Write for 1–3 minutes.)

Day 19
- What I am grateful for (personal characteristics) and why? (Write for 1–3 minutes)

Day 19

- Whom and how I will serve today, and why? (Write for 1–3 minutes.)

Day 19

- What would it take to safely, happily, healthfully, and easily; experience, do, share, be? (Write 1-3 minutes)

- In ten words or less write what you are noticing about yourself from doing these writing exercises.

- Now touch your hand to the left side of your sternum over your heart and read out loud what you wrote this morning. Do this while laughing out loud to cultivate a warm heart for investing in being more yourself.

Day 20 Date: _____
• What I Love About Myself & Others, and Why? (Write for 1–3 minutes.)

Day 20

- What I am grateful for (personal characteristics) and why? (Write for 1–3 minutes.)

Day 20

• Whom and how I will serve today, and why? (Write for 1–3 minutes.)

Day 20

- What would it take to safely, happily, healthfully, and easily; experience, do, share, be? (Write 1-3 minutes)

- In ten words or less write what you are noticing about yourself from doing these writing exercises.

- Now touch your hand to the left side of your sternum over your heart and read out loud what you wrote this morning. Do this while laughing out loud to cultivate a warm heart for investing in being more yourself.

Day 21 Date: _____

• What I Love About Myself & Others, and Why? (Write for 1–3 minutes.)

Day 21

- What I am grateful for (personal characteristics) and why? (Write for 1–3 minutes.)

Day 21

- Whom and how I will serve today, and why? (Write for 1–3 minutes.)

Day 21

- What would it take to safely, happily, healthfully, and easily; experience, do, share, be? (Write 1-3 minutes)

- In ten words or less write what you are noticing about yourself from doing these writing exercises.

- Now touch your hand to the left side of your sternum over your heart and read out loud what you wrote this morning. Do this while laughing out loud to cultivate a warm heart for investing in being more yourself.

Congratulations! This is the 21st day of What's Your Dream Morning Routine!! How has your self-image changed? How do you view yourself creating and manifesting your dreams?

(Write your answer)

To continue this Morning Routinen write the outline of WYDMR in a journal or small 8X5 college rule, 80 sheet spiral note book and continue to continue strengthening your new self-image.

Thanks very much for investing in this morning routine to create your dreams of health, wealth and relationships. May you live the life of your dreams. May all our dreams come true.

References

Video References (VR)

1. Chicken Soup for the Soul series author Jack Canfield shows you how to…
Write A Book In 2017 And
Make It A Big Success
http://www.bestsellerblueprint.com/how-to-write-a-book/
Copyright © by Jack Canfield, Steve Harrison and Bradley Communications Corp. All rights reserved

2. "Bruce Lee's Top 10 Rules For Success"
Evan Carmichael
Published on Jul 12, 2015 https://www.youtube.com/watch?v=u7tL8fK6tjA @ 2:30

3. "Bruce Lee's Top 10 Rules For Success"
Evan Carmichael
Published on Jul 12, 2015 https://www.youtube.com/watch?v=u7tL8fK6tjA @ 3:13

4. Will Smith 60 Minutes Interview https://www.cbsnews.com/video/will-smith/ © 2018 CBS Interactive Inc. All rights reserved.

5. What is the Happiness Advantage? by Shawn Achor, https://www.youtube.com/watch?v=TBRy3QrRGFI
Shawn Achor
Published on Mar 2, 2011
This video highlights a new DVD program based on Shawn Achor's "The Happiness Advantage." To learn more about the book, please visit: http://www.happinessadvantage.com

6. Be Unrealistic and the Best of Will Smith MOTIVATION - #MentorMeWill, https://www.youtube.com/watch?v=UptTQxfj9XI&t=771s
Evan Carmichael
Published on Jul 23, 2016
(VR 7) Full Speech: Jim Carrey's Commencement Address at the 2014 MUM Graduation (https://www.youtube.com/watch?v=V80-gPkpH6M)
Maharishi University of Management
Published on May 30, 2014
8. How to Manifest Rain, Out Of Thin Air! (How to Pray) https://www.youtube.com/watch?v=_u6YcB4c0Y&t=3s&index=86&list=WL
RBabaji
Published on Sep 15, 2010
9. The Art Of Fighting Without Fighting https://www.youtube.com/watch?v=o_Ycw0d_Uow SidTheFish
Published on Oct 3, 2006
10. Allen Watts ~ You Suffer Because You Enjoy it, https://www.youtube.com/watch?v=48JEnQ1kJnc, Willie Study Yourself, January 9, 2014

Book References (BR)

1. Dalai Lama XIV: *How to See Yourself as You Really Are* (Paperback); Atria Books; Reprint edition (November 6, 2007) Jeffrey Hopkins Ph.D. (Editor, Translator)

2. Happiness is when what you think, what you say, and what you do are in harmony. Mahatma Gandhi, as quoted in *Humor, Play, & Laughter : Stress-proofing Life with Your Kids* (1998) by Joseph A. Michelli, p. 88.
3. Gregg Braden: Jul 26, 2016 *Secrets of the Lost Mode of Prayer: The Hidden Power of Beauty, Blessing, Wisdom, and Hurt.* Hay House, Inc, Hay House, Inc. P.O. Box 5100 Carlsbad, CA 92018-5100
4. Dr. Ronald E. Reggio PH.D. Cutting-Edge Leadership *There's Magic in Your Smile; How smiling affects your brain, Psychology Today,* June 25, 2012 Psychology Today © 2018 Sussex Publishers
5. Bendon Burchard, *High Performance Habits: How Extraordinary People Become That Way,* 9-19-17, Hay House is a New Thought and self-help publisher founded in 1984 by author Louise Hay, when she self-published her books Heal Your Body and You Can Heal Your Life. Carlsbad, CA.
6. Elkhart Tolle, *Stillness Speaks,* Hardcover: 144 pages Publisher: New World Library (August 2003)
7. Marcus Buckingham, Donald O. Clifton, *Now Discover Your Strengths,* The Free Press A Division of Simon U Schuster Inc. 1230 Avenue of the Americas New York, NY 10020. Copyright 2001 by The Gallup Organization All rights reserved, including the right of reproduction in whole or in part in any form.

Web References (WR)

1. Intention https://en.wikipedia.org/wiki/Intention This page was last edited on 17 April 2018, at 00:39. Text is available under the Creative Commons Attribution-ShareAlike License; additional terms may apply. By using this site, you agree to the Terms of Use and Privacy Policy. Wikipedia® is a registered trademark of the Wikimedia Foundation, Inc., a non-profit organization.

2. Lama Zopa Rinpoche Quotes https://fpmt.org/teachers/zopa/quotes/ Copyright ©2018 FPMT Inc. FPMT 1632 SE 11th Avenue Portland, OR 97214-4702 USA

3. http://www.shawnachor.com/ Shawn Achor © 2 0 1 8 Shawn Achor All Rights Reserved

4. OPRAH.COM http://www.oprah.com/quote/the-happiness-you-feel-is-in-direct-proportion-to_1 OPRAH IS A REGISTERED TRADEMARK OF HARPO, INC. ALL RIGHTS RESERVED © 2017 HARPO PRODUCTIONS, INC. ALL RIGHTS RESERVED.

5. Health https://en.wikipedia.org/wiki/Health This page was last edited on 14 April 2018, at 19:03. Text is available under the Creative Commons Attribution-ShareAlike License; additional terms may apply. By using this site, you agree to the Terms of Use and Privacy Policy. Wikipedia® is a registered trademark of the Wikimedia Foundation, Inc., a non-profit organization.

6. Wealth https://en.wikipedia.org/wiki/Wealth This page was last edited on 2 April 2018, at 03:25. Text is available under the Creative Commons Attribution-ShareAlike License; additional terms may apply. By using this site, you agree to the Terms of Use and Privacy Policy. Wikipedia® is a registered trademark of the Wikimedia Foundation, Inc., a non-profit organization.
7. His Holiness the 14th Dalai Lama of Tibet www.dalailama.com/messages/compassion-and-human-values/compassion ALL CONTENT COPYRIGHT © THE OFFICE OF HIS HOLINESS THE DALAI LAMA
8. Healthy Hydration, http://www.projectwet.org/sites/default/files/content/documents/hydration-activities.pdf
9. OWN Life Classes, *21 Days to a Happier Life, 21 Days to inspire Happiness Around You.* https://www.ownlifeclasses.com/pages/shawn-achor
10. Muse Vault: A Collection of Techniques, Philosophies and Daily Inspiration to Aid Us All in the Process of Finding Our True Nirvana. "Gregg Braden on 'the single eye of the heart', compassionate living, and using prayer to become a force of love in this world." March, 13, 2012 https://musevault.wordpress.com/2012/03/13/gregg-braden-on-the-single-eye-of-the-heart-compassionate-living-and-using-prayer-to-become-a-force-of-love-in-this-world/ By MuseVault Blog at WordPress.com.

11. Quotes › Authors › W › Will Smith › If you're not making someone else's... http://www.azquotes.com/quote/521603 AZ QUOTES

Personal References (PR)

(PR 1)

Tom Bilyeu is the co-founder of billion-dollar brand Quest Nutrition and the co-founder and host of Impact Theory. Personally driven to expand people's vision of wellness to a 360-degree view that encompasses body and mind, Tom created Impact Theory to help people develop the skills they will need to improve themselves and the world. Through his content and public speaking, he inspires people around the world to unlock their potential and pursue greatness. Tom was named one of Success Magazine's Top 25 Influential People in 2018 and Entrepreneur of the Year by Secret Entourage in 2016.

Hi Michael,

Thanks for reaching out. Yes, you have permission to use the below quote (slightly adjusted) in your book:

"Imagine you have the choice of any of 1,000 doors. Your job is to close 999 of them."

and congrats on writing the book! Can you send us a copy when it's done?

Best,

Jared Smith

Director of Marketing, Impact Theory

Thanks Kindly Tom Bilyeu, Jared Smith and all of Impact Theory for your support and encouragement.
with kindness
Michael J Gilbertr

(PR 2)
Hi Michael,
Sharon is fine with you using this. Do you have an official permissions for us to sign?
Take Care,
Lily
Lily Cushman
Executive Assistant to Sharon Salzberg

    Thanks to Sharon Salzburg for your consent for me to quote you're CD —*A Cup of Kindness* with Nawang Khechog. This CD helps to clarify causes of happiness.
    With kindness
    Michael J. Gilbert
    Sharon's new book *Real Love: The Art of Mindful Connection* has arrived! Sharon is currently on tour for the book, traveling across the U.S. as well as Europe. (https://www.sharonsalzberg.com)

Thanks kindly to Shawn Achor for your research and sharing your studies of happiness. And for creating a happiness course with Oprah. You have helped me find what I was looking for.
With kindness
Michael J. Gilbert

After spending twelve years at Harvard University, **Shawn Achor** has become one of the world's leading experts on the connection between happiness and success. Shawn is the author of *New York Times* best-selling books *The Happiness Advantage* (2010) and *Before Happiness* (2013). He has now lectured in more than 50 countries speaking to CEOs in China, doctors in Dubai, schoolchildren in South Africa, and farmers in Zimbabwe. (http://goodthinkinc.com/speaking/shawn-achor/)

Thanks to Gregg Braden for your teaching and sharing on how to pray. Your videos have been very inspirational and inspiring especially by sharing the view that our prayers are an offering. This changes desire to generosity by changing a person's view. And doing so is a relief of suffering.
With kindness
Michael J. Gilbert

Gregg Braden New York Times best selling author of *Resilience From The Heart, Fractal Time, The God Code* and *The Divine Marix* and is a 2015 nominee of the prestigious Templeton Award. (https://www.greggbraden.com/about-gregg-braden/what-people-are-saying/)

1. Missing Links Interview with Gregg Braden - Gaia Published on Dec 28, 2016 www.gaia.com/missinglinks (http://www.youtube.com/watch?v=4Kbx9MdnRXg)

Thanks kindly to Jack Canfield, Steve Harrison, and everyone at your Best-Seller-Blueprint program. This course has been an amazing resource for creating this book (Best Seller to Be.).

With Kindness
Michael J. Gilbert

Jack Canfield is an award-winning speaker and an internationally recognized leader in personal development and peak performance strategies. For over 40 years, he has been teaching entrepreneurs, educators, corporate leaders, and people from all walks of life how to create the life they desire. As the beloved originator of the *Chicken Soup for the Soul*® series, he's taught millions of individuals his modernized formulas for success, and now certifies trainers in the Canfield Methodology all over the world. www.jackcanfield.com
http://www.bestsellerblueprintcourse.com/fullcourse.htm

Thanks kindly to Vishen Lakhiani for creating Mind Valley. Your courses have created a new kind of education for me and have been an excellent addition to learning how to create this book and see myself as an author.

With kindness

Michael J. Gilbert

Vishen Lakhiani was born and raised in Kuala Lumpur, Malaysia, Vishen Lakhiani founded Mindvalley in 2003 while he was living in New York, after discovering the benefits of mindfulness and meditation to help him cope with a stressful sales career. He made it his mission to build one of the best workplaces in the world in Malaysia, despite the odds. Today, Vishen leads a 200-strong team of over 40 nationalities under a multi award-winning company culture. (http://www.mindvalley.com/vishen.html)

Thanks to Bruce and Linda Lee for sharing *Tao of Jeet Kune Do* (1975) Ohara Publications, Inc

Thanks to Stefan Pylarinos for creating your program *Morning Ritual Mastery Program*. When I was living in my car I found this program and used it to create my morning ritual.

With kindness

Michael J. Gilbert

Stefan Pylarinos a 7-figure internet entrepreneur, life and business coach, fitness enthusiast, and world traveler with an obsession to live life to the fullest and fulfilling my potential as a human being. (http://projectlifemastery.com/about/)

Thanks to Christi Marie Sheldon for sharing your "Unlimited Abundance Course" with Mind Valley to also share. This course is great to develop a more positive attitude.

With Kindness
Michael J. Gilbert

Hi, my name is Christie Marie Sheldon and I love to use my Spiritual Gifts to help guide people manifest the reality of their dreams. I often do this by helping them open up their awareness, raise their energetic frequency and learn to use their own Spiritual Gifts so they can continue helping themselves. (christiesheldon.com)

Thanks kindly to Brendon Burchard for your valuable research that people can use as inspiration to live a fulfilling life. Your work and research has helped me live a more inspired life. It's a privilege to have your support.

With kindness
Michael J. Gilbert

Brendon Burchard is the world's leading high performance coach, a 3-time *New York Times* bestselling author, and one of the most-watched, quoted, and followed personal development trainers in history. (https://brendon.com)

Some of Brendon Burchard's books include:

The Motivation Manifesto, 2014.

The Charge: Activating the Ten Human Drives That Make You Feel Alive 2012

High Performance Habits: How Extraordinary People Become that way, 2017

website: www.expertsacademy.com, brendon.com, highperformanceacademy.com

Thanks to Will Smith for being an inspirational speaker. Your interviews with Oprah, Sixty Minutes and more, are inspiring because you're showing people we can all live the life of our dreams.

With kindness

Michael J. Gilbert

Thanks to Echart Tolle for sharing your books and videos to point out what everyone is looking for, this moment. And thanks for reading this right now.

With kindness

Michael J. Gilbert

Eckhart is a spiritual teacher and author who was born in Germany and educated at the Universities of London and Cambridge. At the age of 29, a profound inner transformation radically changed the course of his life. The next few years were devoted to understanding, integrating and deepening that transformation, which marked the beginning of an intense inward journey. Later, he began to work in London with individuals and small groups as a counselor and spiritual teacher. Eckhart shares his time between British Columbia, Canada and California. Eckhart Tolle is the author of the #1 *New York Times* bestseller *The Power of Now* (translated into 33 languages) and the highly acclaimed follow-up A *New Earth*, which are widely regarded as two of the most influential spiritual books of our time. (http://eckharttolle.com/about/eckhart/)

Thanks to Yoda for teaching the ways of the force.
With kindness
Michael J. Gilbert

Thanks to Oprah Winfrey for being an inspiration for people to be themselves.
With Kindness
Michael J. Gilbert

Michael's Words of Wisdom (MWW)

"It's not what you do, it's how often you do it."

"All our dreams come true from happiness, not the other way around."

"Happiness or unhappiness come from how a person is *being* with their moment."

"Knowing how to create happiness is knowing thyself."

"Happiness is not a feeling, it's a byproduct of our actions. When we start striving for a feeling, that's when we create addictions."

"The road to happiness is paved with necessity."

"Sanity is overrated."

"Are your dreams fitting into someone else's dreams for you, or is your life growing into your dreams?"

"Am I unhappy about being unhappy or happy about my intention to create happiness while being unhappy?"

"Happiness is recognizing our true self as space, emptiness, unlimited potential."

"The creation from your intention and your intention is not just yours alone."

"A person does not change oneself, a person changes how they treat themselves."

"Does our intention come from how we treat our suffering?"

"Willingness to feel the pain of negative self-beliefs is self-compassion."

"Just like unhappiness, happiness needs care too."

"Cause someone to suffer, and one may or may not earn someone's respect. Relieve someone's suffering, and you will earn self-respect."

"Someone is praying for something I'm taking for granted."

"The experience of gratitude includes being grateful for what you don't have and didn't want."

"The more we enjoy what we are sharing, the more we will enjoy what we have."

"Waking up = making the decision to live your dreams."

"Humility is the appreciation of one's own positive qualities learned from someone else."

"It's my favorite day of the year —it's today! (Tomorrow is over-rated, yesterday is for has-beens.)"

"Would writing about what you love every morning give your life more sense of direction and meaning?"

"When happiness comes easy, it can be taken for granted."

"Happiness is created from loving and enjoying what we're sharing with other people."

"Gratitude is appreciating what you can do, and doing it!"

"Doing hard things, working hard, is overrated. Do what you love and appreciating the ease in this, is underrated."

"I bless the causes of my happiness."

"I am the relief of my suffering."

"The key to my happiness is me."

"How am I treating my consciousness?"

"Becoming a happier person is personal growth."

"Cleaning is the practice of self respect."

"The drive to be "better" comes from not knowing oneself. When we know who we are we strive to know and treat ourselves better."

"Turning adversity into opportunity is overrated. Turning enjoyment into opportunity is underrated."

"Life only gets better with gratitude. Gratitude comes from patience."

"Self enjoyment is my sanctuary and my sanctuary is my prison."

"Practice abundance by offering what you want:
- If lonely, bless everyone with love.
- If suffering, bless everyone with compassion.
- If anxious, bless everyone with content.
- If afraid, bless everyone with joy.
- If poor, bless everyone with gratitude.
- If bored, bless everyone with humor."

"It's human nature to explore, start with yourself. What's Your Dream?"

"May our dreams coming true be free of suffering and the causes of suffering."

"**A dream is a wish to create our desires with the positive energy of love, joy, compassion, equanimity, content and gratitude.**"

Thanks very kindly for your investment in this book.

www.ingramcontent.com/pod-product-compliance
Lightning Source LLC
Chambersburg PA
CBHW051343040426
42453CB00007B/378